sunshine
cocktails

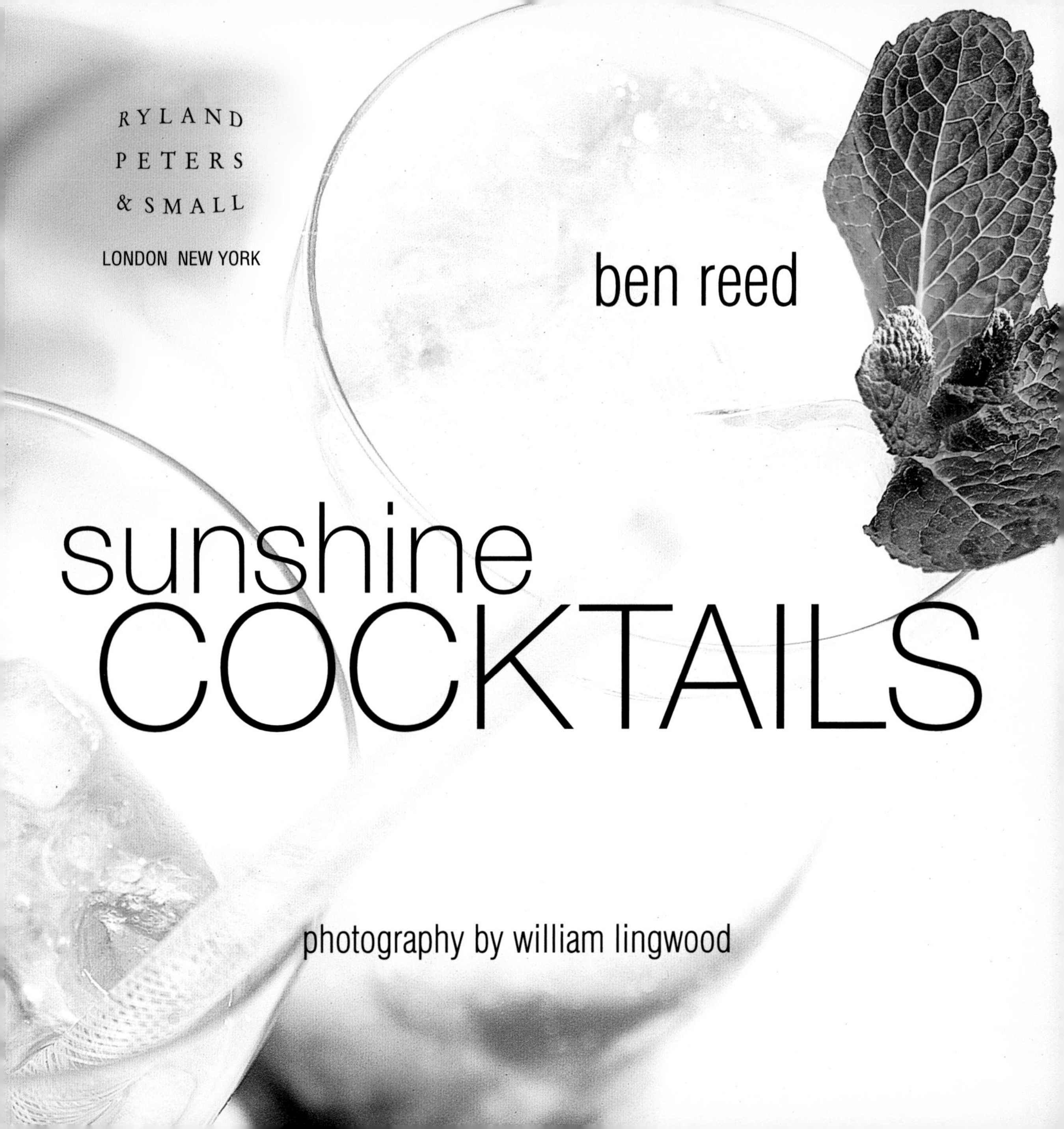

RYLAND
PETERS
& SMALL

LONDON NEW YORK

ben reed

sunshine
COCKTAILS

photography by william lingwood

Senior Designers Catherine Griffin and Anna Murphy

Editor Miriam Hyslop

Production Gavin Bradshaw

Art Director Gabriella Le Grazie

Publishing Director Alison Starling

Mixologist Ben Reed

Stylist Helen Trent

First published in the United States in 2005 by
Ryland Peters & Small, Inc.
519 Broadway, 5th Floor
New York NY 10012
www.rylandpeters.com

10 9 8 7 6 5 4 3 2 1

Printed in China.

Ben Reed's recipes have been published previously in various titles from
Ryland Peters & Small.

Library of Congress Cataloging-in-Publication Data

Reed, Ben.
  Sunshine cocktails / by Ben Reed ; photography by William Lingwood.
    p. cm.
  Includes index.
  ISBN 1-84172-836-5
  1. Cocktails. I. Title.
  TX951.R35528 2005
  641.8'74--dc22
                    2004019821

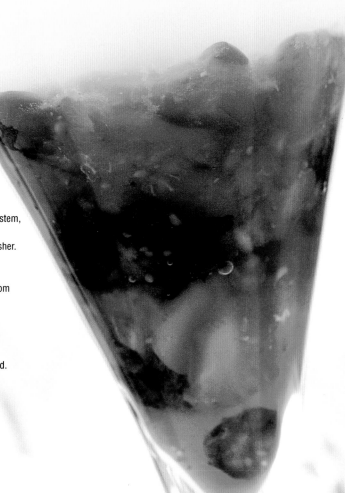

contents

introduction

You might think that cocktails are the reserve of special events such as anniversaries and birthdays. I believe, however, that there's a cocktail for every occasion—including a hot summer's day.

While people tend to equate cocktails with the plush interiors of hotel bars and cocktail lounges, cocktails can be enjoyed equally in the comfort of one's own home or garden. With a bit of innovation, cocktails can be mixed over ice, strained into a thermos, and taken to the park or the beach (he says wistfully).

In *Sunshine Cocktails*, I have selected 60 of my favorite refreshing drinks. Some are long and fruity, others are charged with champagne for a touch of decadence, and more still are short, ice cold, with a citrus tang.

The sunshine changes everyone's outlook on life. When the sun shines people tend to become more adventurous, and this is often reflected in their choice of drink. Remember those sickly flavored daiquiris that you enjoyed so much on vacation in the Caribbean? Can you imagine drinking them in your local bar? Thought not..! With the recipes in this book, however, you can recapture that holiday feeling wherever you are. The Caipirinha, despite its almost unpronounceable name, is one of the simplest drinks to make at home (although

it can be a bit time consuming!). All you need is a lime, some sugar, and cachaça (a spirit indigenous to Brazil) and you can create your own Caipirinha. The Pimm's Cocktail is also refreshing and easy to prepare. Yet how many of you would remember to add a slice of cucumber? Without the cucumber the drink doesn't taste as good as it could. Read on, and you'll discover the best way to create this quintessentailly English drink.

Try using the ripest, freshest ingredients in a Fresh and Fruity cocktail—from a long cool Raspberry Rickey to a minty Mojito. If you like a drink that packs a punch, the Feisty selection features recipes for strong, short drinks including the Classic Margarita and Orange Daiquiri. For relaxed entertaining there are Fizzy cocktails bound to bring a sparkle to any occasion. Try the irresistible combination of fruit and fizz in the Bellini, or the delicate balance of flavors in a Ginger Champagne. With gorgeous recipes for non-alcoholic drinks, in the Softies section, such as the Cranberry Cooler, St. Clement's, and Iced Tea there is a cocktail guaranteed to delight your tastebuds.

There are rules that I ask you to adhere to whenever making a summer cocktail. First, make the drink as cold as possible. This is a fairly standard rule when making cocktails, but during those sunshine days its difficult to keep drinks cool, so always stock up with fresh ice. If using home-made ice, remember to use mineral water. Always add as much ice as will fit into the glass. The more ice in the glass, the colder the glass and therefore the slower the ice melts.

Secondly, balance the flavors in your drinks with care—oversweet cocktails just won't do. The principle is as follows; the base liquor should provide the bulk of the taste and the addition of sweet and sour should provide the balance.

Despite the frivolity and obvious jollity of drinking in the sun, do bear in mind that alcohol and sunshine aren't always the best of friends, so do take care and ensure you are well hydrated at all times by drinking plenty of water.

Whatever the weather, this marvelous book is a treat you can enjoy at home, in the garden, or on a tropical beach!

equipment and techniques

EQUIPMENT The first thing any aspiring bartender should acquire is a **jigger**. Too many professional bartenders regard the jigger as a tool for the novice—their guesswork results in many delicate cocktails being ruined. The modern dual-measure jigger measures both one ounce and two ounces (a double and a single measure). The **shaker** is the second most important piece of equipment for a bartender. The Boston Shaker, half stainless steel, half glass, is my preference for a stylish performance but the more orthodox shaker with the inbuilt strainer works equally well. The **barspoon**, with its long spiralling handle, is useful for stirring drinks and for the gentle pouring required for **layering** drinks. The "wrong," flat end can be used for muddling or crushing herbs, etc. A **muddler**, a wooden pestle for mixing or crushing sugar cubes, limes, and herbs, and the **bartender's friend** for opening cans and removing corks and bottle caps, are also handy. A **mixing glass** with strainer is used for making drinks that are stirred, not shaken. **Straws** are useful to hygienically test your drink before you serve (see the pipette method). Other useful but not essential accessories include an **ice bucket**, **ice tongs**, **blender**, and a **juice squeezer**.

TECHNIQUES There are six basic ways of creating a cocktail: building, blending, shaking, stirring over ice, layering, and muddling. Whichever method you are using, accurately measure the ingredients first to get that all-important balance of tastes right. If you would rather try guesswork just see how much practice it takes to get the quantity right to fill the glass exactly—I still have problems in that department! The process

ESSENTIAL EQUIPMENT
- jigger
- shaker
- barspoon
- muddler
- bartender's friend
- mixing glass
- ice

USEFUL EQUIPMENT
- straws
- ice bucket
- ice tongs
- blender
- juice squeezer
- a knife
- swizzle sticks

of **building** a cocktail just requires adding the measured ingredients to the appropriate glass, with ice, and giving it a quick stir before serving. The **blending** method involves pouring all the ingredients into a blender, adding crushed ice and flicking the switch. Using a **shaker** is the most enjoyable way to mix a cocktail, both for you and your guests. Add the ingredients to the shaker and fill it with ice. The shaking movement should be sharp and fairly assertive, but do remember to keep your hands on both parts of the shaker or at least a finger on the cap. Drinks containing cream and juices should be shaken for slightly longer than the usual ten seconds. **Stirring** is the best method when you want to retain the clarity and strength of the spirits. Use an ice-filled mixing glass and stir carefully to avoid chipping the ice and diluting the drink. Frost your serving glasses by leaving them in the freezer for an hour before use. The **muddling** technique involves using the flat end of a barspoon or a muddler to mix or crush ingredients such as fruit or herbs and allow the flavors to be released gently. The **pipette method** is used to taste the drink before serving. Submerge a straw in to your drink, cover the tip with your finger to create a vacuum. Take the straw from the drink and suck the liquid from the straw.

GLASSES The traditional **martini glass** is a very familiar icon, with its open face and slim stem. The **cocktail glass** is similar to the martini glass but with a slightly rounded bowl. The **rocks** or **old-fashioned glass** is a squat, straight-sided glass, which sits on a heavy base. The **highball** and the **collins glasses** come in various sizes but they are all tall, slim glasses designed to keep a long drink fresh and cold. The **champagne flute** is perfect for keeping the sparkle in your champagne cocktails. It should be elegant and long-stemmed, with a narrow rim to enhance the delicacy of the drink. The **margarita coupette** and **hurricane glass** often hold margaritas and frozen punches.

fresh and fruity

moscow mule

The creation of the Moscow Mule woke us up to the Godsend that is ginger beer. It lends the Mule its legendary kick and an easy spiciness. (For just a nudge rather than a kick, use ginger ale).

1 ¾ oz. vodka
½ lime
ginger beer, to top up

Pour the vodka into a highball glass filled with ice. Squeeze the lime, cut into four, into the glass and drop it in. Top with ginger beer and stir with a barspoon. Serve with a straw.

strawberry mule

Perfect for an afternoon in the sun. Try substituting dark rum or bourbon for the vodka, for a delicious alternative.

2 thin slices fresh ginger
3 fresh strawberries, plus 1 to garnish
1 ¾ oz. vodka
½ oz. crème de fraise de bois
a dash of simple syrup
ginger beer, to top up

Muddle together the ginger and the strawberries in a mixing glass. Add the vodka, fraise de bois, and simple syrup, and shake then strain through a fine mesh strainer into a highball glass filled with ice. Top with ginger beer, stir, and serve garnished with a strawberry.

brazilian mule

Try this variation of the Moscow Mule—great for an after-dinner drink.

1 oz. vodka
½ oz. peppermint schnapps
½ oz. Stone's Ginger Wine
1 oz. espresso coffee
a dash of simple syrup
ginger beer, to top up
2 coffee beans, to garnish

Add the vodka, peppermint schnapps, and ginger wine to an ice-filled shaker. Pour in the espresso coffee and simple syrup to taste. Shake, and strain into a highball glass filled with ice, and top with ginger beer. Garnish with two coffee beans.

planter's punch

A Planter's Punch recipe can never be forgotten since Myers very kindly puts the recipe on the back label of its rum bottle. A great favorite for parties because it can be made in advance.

1 ¾ oz. Myers rum
juice of ½ lemon
1 ¾ oz. fresh orange juice
a dash of simple syrup
club soda, to top up
orange slice, to garnish

Pour all the ingredients, except the club soda, into a shaker filled with ice. Shake, and strain into an ice-filled highball glass. Top up with club soda and garnish with a slice of orange.

t-punch

Perfect for a hot summer day, the T-Punch is a refreshing drink which can be made with more lime or more sugar, according to taste.

1 brown sugar cube
1 lime
1 ¾ oz. white rum
soda water, to top up (optional)

Place the sugar cube in the bottom of an old-fashioned glass. Cut the lime into eighths, squeeze into the glass, and drop them in. Pound with a pestle to break up the sugar. Add the rum and ice, then top up with club soda. Stir and serve.

rum runner

The Rum Runner is a delicious example of rum's affinity with fresh juices as we've seen over the years in the classic Tiki cocktails and punches of Don the Beachcomber.

1 oz. white rum
1 oz. dark rum
juice of ½ lime
½ oz. simple syrup
⅔ cup fresh pineapple juice

Shake all the ingredients sharply with ice in a shaker, then strain into a highball glass filled with crushed ice.

dark and stormy

One of my favorite long cocktails—warm and comforting with its dark rum base, but also zingy and refreshing with the tried and tested partnership of lime and ginger beer.

1 ¾ oz. dark rum
spicy ginger beer, to top up
4 lime wedges

Build the rum and ginger beer into a rocks glass filled with ice. Squeeze the limes, and drop the husks into the glass. Stir gently and serve.

cuba libre

One of the most famous of all rum-based drinks, this was reputed to have been invented by an army officer in Cuba shortly after Coca Cola was first produced in the 1890s.

1 ¾ oz. white rum
½ lime
cola, to top up

Pour the rum into a highball glass filled with ice. Cut the lime into four, squeeze into the glass, and drop the wedges in. Top with cola and serve with straws.

blueberry amaretto sour

If you want to add that special touch to your cocktail and don't mind putting in a bit of work, then infusing blueberries in your amaretto is well worth the effort.

2 oz. blueberry-infused amaretto (see below)
1 oz. lemon juice
½ oz. simple syrup
lemon slice and 2 blueberries, to garnish

Blueberry-infused amaretto: Pierce ten blueberries with a knife and place them in a bottle of amaretto. Leave them for a few days, then taste. You may want to strain the mixture before using it.

Add all the ingredients to a shaker filled with ice, shake sharply, and strain into a rocks glass filled with ice. Garnish with two blueberries and a lemon slice.

gin bramble

This is a perfect cocktail for
drinking on a sunny deck in
the cool of early evening.

1 ¾ oz. gin
1 oz. fresh lemon juice
½ oz. simple syrup
2 teaspoons crème de mure
lemon slice and blackberry, to garnish

Add the gin, lemon juice, and simple
syrup to a shaker filled with ice. Shake
the mixture and strain into a sling glass.
Fill with crushed ice and pour in the
crème de mure gently so that the liquid
sinks to the bottom of the cocktail.
Garnish with a slice of lemon and
a fresh blackberry.

french martini

This martini is great for parties since it is light and creamy, and simple to make in bulk. Shake this one hard when preparing it and you will be rewarded with a thick white froth on the surface of the drink.

1 ¾ oz. vodka
a large dash of Chambord or crème de mure
2 ½ oz. fresh pineapple juice

Add all the ingredients to a shaker filled with ice, shake sharply, and strain into a frosted martini glass.

citrus martini

The Citrus Martini needs to be shaken hard to take the edge off the lemon. Try substituting lime for lemon for a slightly more tart variation.

2 oz. Cytryonowka vodka
1 oz. lemon juice
1 oz. Cointreau
a dash of simple syrup
lemon zest, to garnish

Add all the ingredients to a shaker filled with ice, shake sharply, and strain into a frosted martini glass. Garnish with the lemon zest.

cherry martini

This martini can also be made using the juice from canned cherries—it may not sound so nice on paper, but wait until you taste it! For a delicious variation, try using the juice from canned lychees—another winner!

3 pitted fresh cherries
1 ¾ oz. vodka
1 ¾ oz. thick cherry juice
a dash of maraschino

Crush the cherries in a shaker using the flat end of a barspoon. Add ice and the remaining ingredients, shake sharply, and strain through a fine mesh strainer into a frosted martini glass.

raspberry martini

This old favorite of mine should be quite thick in consistency, so if you aren't using purée, use a handful of raspberries to ensure it flows down your throat like molasses in January.

1 ¾ oz. vodka
a dash of crème de framboise
a dash of orange bitters
½ oz. raspberry purée
2 fresh raspberries, to garnish

Shake all the ingredients in a shaker filled with ice and strain into a frosted martini glass. Garnish with two fresh raspberries.

prickly pear margarita

The prickly pear has become *de rigueur* in cocktails, and makes a great addition to the margarita.

1 ¾ oz. silver tequila

¾ oz. triple sec

¾ oz. lime juice

a dash of grenadine

1 oz. prickly pear purée

thin pear slice, to garnish

Add all the ingredients to a shaker filled with ice. Shake sharply, and strain into a frosted margarita glass. Garnish with a sliver of pear.

berry margarita

Anything from strawberries or cranberries, to blueberries or raspberries can be used in this recipe. Choose your own combination of seasonal berries for subtle variations.

1 ¾ oz. gold tequila

¾ oz. triple sec

¾ oz. fresh lime juice

a dash of crème de mure

seasonal berries of your choice, plus extra to garnish

Add all the ingredients to a blender. Add two scoops of crushed ice and blend for 20 seconds. Pour into a margarita coupette and garnish with berries.

green iguana

The combination of melon and tequila work perfectly here. I have chosen to use Midori (a melon-flavored liqueur) in this recipe since fresh melon doesn't have the necessary sweetness to balance the drink.

1 oz. Sauza Hornitos tequila
¾ oz. Midori
¾ oz. fresh lime juice
¾ oz. Cointreau
lime wedge, to garnish

Add all the ingredients to a shaker filled with ice. Shake sharply. Strain into a rocks glass.

blue moon

I'm not a man to hold grudges but I'm not a huge
fan of blue cocktails, they tend to contain blue
Curaçao for its color rather than its taste. In the Blue
Moon, however, blue Curaçao is valid, as the liqueur
is orange-flavoured Curaçao, much like triple sec.

2 oz. Sauza Hornitos tequila
1 oz. blue Curaçao
tablespoon fresh lime juice
2 scoops lemon sherbet

Add all the ingredients to a blender. Blend for 20 seconds
and pour into a margarita glass.

mojito

Guaranteed to whisk you away
to warmer, more tropical climes,
the Mojito emerged in London
over the summer of 1998 as the
thinking man's refreshing tipple.

5 mint sprigs
1 ¾ oz. golden rum
a dash of fresh lime juice
2 dashes of simple syrup
club soda, to top up

Put the mint in a highball glass, add
the rum, lime juice and simple syrup,
and pound with a barspoon until
the aroma of the mint is released.
Add crushed ice and stir vigorously
until the mixture and the mint is
spread evenly. Top with club soda
and stir again. Serve with straws.

horse's neck

Don't get too carried away trying to get the spiral of lemon either too long or too similar to a horse's neck—after all, it's how the drink tastes that's important!

1 ¾ oz. bourbon
ginger ale, to top up
lemon spiral, to garnish

Build the ingredients in a highball glass filled with ice. Drape the lemon spiral into the glass and over the edge. Serve with two straws.

pimm's cup

This cocktail is my one concession to the addition of elaborate fruit salad-type garnishes to a drink—anything goes with the Pimm's! Surprisingly, the tastiest addition to this drink is the cucumber, but try adding some sliced apple, too.

1 ¾ oz.Pimm's No 1
8 oz. lemon soda (e.g., 7-Up)
⅓ cup ginger beer
cucumber slice
lemon slice
orange slice
fresh strawberry
mint sprig

Build all the ingredients in a highball glass filled with ice. Stir gently and serve with two straws.

madras

The Madras is especially refreshing when created with fresh orange juice.

1 ¾ oz. vodka
cranberry juice, to top up
fresh orange juice, to top up
orange slice, to garnish

Pour the vodka into a highball glass filled with ice. Top with equal amounts of cranberry juice and orange juice and garnish with an orange slice. Serve with a straw.

tropical breeze

A twist on the breeze format using flavored vodka and fresh juices. There are a number of variations on this theme due to the ever-growing number of flavored vodkas on the market these days.

1 ¾ oz. Wyborowa Melon vodka
cranberry juice, to top up
fresh grapefruit juice, to top up

Pour the melon-flavored vodka into a highball glass filled with ice. Top with equal amounts of cranberry and fresh grapefruit juice.

sea breeze

The Sea Breeze is a modern, thirst-quenching variation on the classic Screwdriver. The cranberry juice lends a light, fruity, refreshing quality and combines with the bitter grapefruit juice, making it very popular with people who don't really enjoy the taste of alcohol.

1 ¾ oz. vodka
5 oz. cranberry juice
1 ½ oz. fresh grapefruit juice
lime wedge, to garnish

Pour the vodka into a highball glass filled with ice. Fill the glass three-quarter full with cranberry juice, and top with fresh grapefruit juice. Garnish with a lime wedge and serve with a straw.

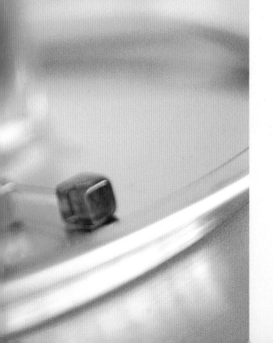

claret cobbler

A classic cocktail that can take whatever time throws at it. Choose red Bordeaux or Cabernet-Merlot blends for the claret.

lemon slice
lime wedge
orange wheel
1 oz. claret or port
¾ oz. vodka
¾ oz. crème de framboise

Muddle the fruit in a shaker. Add the remaining ingredients, shake sharply and strain through a fine mesh strainer into a rocks glass.

champagne cobbler

Champagne works with many complex flavors. If the fruit is not as ripe as it could be, add a dash more simple syrup to encourage the flavor.

pineapple slice
orange wheel
lemon wheel
a dash of simple syrup
champagne, to top up
mint sprig, to garnish

Muddle the fruit together in a rocks glass. Add crushed ice and the simple syrup, and gently top with champagne. Stir gently, and garnish with a mint sprig.

port cobbler

Port has long been excluded from the world of contemporary cocktails simply because it is perceived as fuddy duddy. However, its full flavor works well in many cocktails.

orange wheel
lemon wheel
pineapple slice, plus 1 to garnish
2 ½ oz. ruby port
2 dashes of orange curaçao

Muddle the fruit in a mixing glass, add the other ingredients, and stir well. Strain into a rocks glass filled with crushed ice. Garnish with a pineapple slice, and serve.

a colada

A sweet, creamy drink which, for a time, epitomized the kind of cocktail that "real" cocktail drinkers disapproved of (compare a Piña Colada with a Dry Martini!). Today, cocktails are for everyone so there's no shame in ordering a Piña Colada at the bar.

2 oz. golden rum
1 oz. coconut cream
½ oz. cream
1 oz. fresh pineapple juice
pineapple slice, to garnish

Put all the ingredients in a blender, add a scoop of crushed ice, and blend. Pour into a hurricane or highball glass, and garnish with a thick slice of pineapple.

honey colada

Try the Honey Colada variation for a sweet surprise lurking at the bottom of the glass—only for the very sweet-toothed! Alternatively, use the Mexican liqueur Kahlúa as the base, for a light coffee taste.

For a Honey Colada, add two barspoons of honey or simple syrup to a freshly made Piña Colada.

tequila colada

This variation slips down the throat as easily as its name rolls off the tongue. Ensure this drink has the right consistency (light and fluffy) by adding crushed ice bit by bit to the blender.

1 ¾ oz. gold tequila
2 oz. coconut cream
½ oz. heavy cream
5 oz. pineapple juice
pineapple slice, to garnish

Add all the ingredients to a blender along with two scoops of crushed ice. Blend for 20 seconds. Pour into a hurricane glass and garnish with a pineapple slice.

black bird

The Black Bird is not a spur-of-the-moment type of drink. The work put in beforehand is in equal proportion to the look of amazement on its drinker's face. The Cointreau and the brandy in the mix draw all the juices out of the berries and they combine with the alcohol in a most un-alcoholic way. This is a drink to be wary of.

berry mix:
- 1 cup strawberries
- 1 cup raspberries
- 1 cup blueberries
- 1 cup cranberries
- 1 oz. brandy
- 1 oz. Cointreau
- 2 ½ cups superfine sugar
- 2 oz. lemon vodka
- 1 oz. lemon juice
- ¾ oz. Cointreau

Berry mix: Place all the ingredients in a large bowl, stir once and leave overnight. Stir once more before serving

Place a scoop of berry mix into a frosted martini glass and press down. Pour the remaining ingredients into a shaker filled with ice, shake sharply, then gently strain the mixture into the martini glass.

mai tai

This cocktail has many variations. A thick, dark rum should be used along with all the fruit-based ingredients that lend it its legendary fruitiness.

1 ¾ oz. demerara rum
½ oz. orange curaçao
½ oz. apricot brandy
¾ oz. fresh lemon
¾ oz. fresh lime juice
a dash of Angostura bitters
¾ oz. orgeat syrup
mint sprig, to garnish

Add all the ingredients to a shaker filled with ice, shake, and strain into an ice-filled old-fashioned glass. Garnish with a mint sprig and serve with straws.

peach rickey

I sold a great many Peach Rickeys after devising this cocktail to use up a surplus of peaches ordered by an overenthusiastic bartender. Ripe peaches will yield the best results if you're making your own purée.

1 ¾ oz. vodka
¾ oz. fresh lime juice
½ oz. white peach purée
a dash of crème de pêche
club soda, to top up
thin peach slices, to serve

Build all the ingredients into a highball glass filled with ice. Stir gently and garnish with a thin peach slice or two.

elderflower collins

The botanicals in the gin get a bit of an unexpected boost from the elderflower, making this a delicate cocktail full of floral flavors.

1 ¾ oz. gin
¾ oz. fresh lemon juice
½ oz. elderflower-flavored concentrate
a dash of simple syrup
club soda, to top up
lemon slice, to garnish

Build all the ingredients into a highball glass filled with ice. Stir gently and garnish with a lemon slice.

raspberry rickey

This fresh fruit cooler always appeals due to the nature of the ingredients—there just seems to be something about raspberries in cocktails that everyone enjoys!

4 fresh raspberries, plus 1 to garnish
1 ¾ oz. vodka
¾ oz. fresh lime juice
a dash of Chambord
club soda, to top up

Muddle the raspberries in the bottom of a highball glass. Fill with ice and add the remaining ingredients and stir gently.
Garnish with a fresh raspberry and serve with two straws.

vodka collins

Try the Vodka Collins for a sharp, zingy, thirst quencher on a hot day. Be warned, it's easy to forget there is alcohol in the drink!

1 ¾ oz. Vox vodka
¾ oz. fresh lemon juice
½ oz. simple syrup
club soda, to top up
lemon slice, to garnish

Build the ingredients into a highball glass filled with ice. Stir gently and garnish with a lemon slice. Serve with two straws.

feisty

original daiquiri

This classic cocktail was made famous at the El Floridita restaurant, Havana, early in the 20th century. Once you have found the perfect balance of light rum (traditionally Cuban), sharp citrus juice, and sweet simple syrup, stick to those measurements exactly.

1 ¾ oz. golden rum
1 oz. fresh lime juice
2 teaspoons simple syrup

Pour all the ingredients into an ice-filled shaker. Shake, and strain into a frosted martini glass.

orange daiquiri

The Orange Daiquiri substitutes the sweet Martinique rum called Creole Shrub for the Cuban rum of the Original Daiquiri, so uses a little less simple syrup to keep that delicate balance of sharp and sweet.

1 ¾ oz. Creole Shrub rum
¾ oz. fresh lime juice
1 teaspoon simple syrup

Pour all the ingredients into an ice-filled shaker. Shake, and strain into a frosted martini glass.

caipirinha

Cachaça, a liquor indigenous to Brazil, is distilled directly from the juice of sugar cane. The Caipirinha has made cachaça popular in many countries.

1 lime
2 brown sugar cubes
1 ¾ oz. cachaça
simple syrup, to taste

Cut the lime into eighths, squeeze, and place in an old-fashioned glass with the sugar cubes, then pound well with a pestle. Fill the glass with crushed ice and add the cachaça. Stir vigorously and add simple syrup, to taste. Serve with two straws.

cowboy hoof

The color of this drink alone is worth the effort. Pay attention when straining the mixture since bits of mint sticking to the teeth are never attractive!

12 mint leaves, plus 1 to garnish
2 teaspoons simple syrup
2 ¼ oz. gin

Shake all the ingredients in a shaker filled with ice and strain through a fine mesh strainer into a frosted martini glass. Garnish with a sprig of fresh mint.

margarita

...ung pretenders out there who do not ... the respect it deserves. Margarita ...quila, too much ice, and sweetened, concentrated lime juice instead of fresh lemon or lime juice all contribute to an unacceptable cocktail. Don't let your margaritas be tarred by the same brush!

1 ½ oz. gold tequila
¾ oz. triple sec or Cointreau
juice of ½ lime
salt, for the glass

Shake all the ingredients sharply with cracked ice, then strain into a frosted margarita glass rimmed with salt.

triple gold margarita

Layered with a float of Goldschlager, the Triple Gold Margarita will
bring a touch of splendor to any bar menu. Laced with real 24-carat
gold pieces, Goldschlager is a cinnamon-flavored liqueur that adds
considerably to the depth of taste of the cocktail.

1 ¾ oz. gold tequila
2 teaspoons Cointreau
2 teaspoons Grand Marnier
¾ oz. fresh lime juice
¾ oz. Goldschlager

Add all the ingredients except the Goldschlager to a shaker filled with ice.
Shake sharply and strain into a frosted margarita glass. Float the Goldschlager onto
the surface of the mixture, and serve.

fresca

The Fresca was invented to be served long with lemon soda as a refreshing summer drink, but for every drinker who wants their thirst quenched, there will always be two who want their socks knocked off—and who am I to argue? See opposite for a choice of ingredients.

Add the ingredients to a shaker filled with ice, shake sharply, then strain through a fine mesh strainer into a frosted martini glass. Garnish and serve.

basil and honey

1 ¾ oz. vodka

a dash of lime juice

a dash of grapefruit juice

2 basil sprigs, crushed

1 teaspoon honey

basil leaf, to garnish

orange and pear

1 ¾ oz. vodka

a dash of lime juice

a dash of grapefruit juice

orange slice, crushed

pear slice, crushed

orange zest, to garnish

port and blackberry

1 ¾ oz. vodka

½ oz. port

a dash of lime juice

a dash of grapefruit juice

4 blackberries, plus 2 to garnish

fizzy

champagne cocktail

This cocktail has truly stood the test of time, being as
popular now as when it was sipped by stars of the silver
screen in the 1940s. It's a simple and delicious cocktail
which epitomizes the elegance and sophistication of that
era and still lends the same touch of urbanity (one hopes!)
to those who drink it today.

1 white sugar cube
2 dashes of Angostura bitters
1 oz. brandy
dry champagne, to top up

Place the sugar cube in a champagne flute and moisten with
Angostura bitters. Add the brandy, stir, then gently pour in the
champagne and serve.

bellini

The Bellini originated in Harry's Bar in Venice in the early 1940s and became a favorite among the movers and shakers of chic society. Although there are many variations on this recipe, there is one golden rule for the perfect Bellini—always use fresh, ripe peaches to make the peach juice.

½ fresh peach, skinned
½ oz. crème de pêche
a dash of peach bitters (optional)
champagne, to top up
peach ball, to garnish

Purée the peach in a blender and add to a champagne flute. Pour in the crème de pêche and the peach bitters, and gently top up with champagne, stirring carefully and continuously. Garnish with a peach ball in the bottom of the glass, then serve.

champagne julep

This cocktail works with all types of champagne or sparkling wine. If you have a bottle of bubbly that has been open for a while and lost a bit of its fizz, don't worry, the sugar in the recipe will revitalize it.

5 mint sprigs, plus 1 to garnish
½ oz. simple syrup
a dash of lime juice
champagne, to top up

Muddle the mint, simple syrup, and lime juice together in a highball glass. Add crushed ice and the champagne (gently), and stir. Garnish with a mint sprig and serve.

kir royale

After a shaky start, the Kir Royale is now the epitome of chic sophistication. It started life as the Kir (a variation using acidic white wine instead of champagne) and was labeled *rince cochon* (pig rinse!). Luckily, the wine became less sharp and the drink adopted a more appropriate mantle!

a dash of crème de cassis
champagne, to top up

Add a small dash of crème de cassis to a champagne flute and gently top with champagne. Stir gently and serve.

sloe gin fizz

You may need to play with the balance of flavors in this cocktail. Different brands of sloe gin have different concentrations of sweetness and flavor—as is the case with many liqueurs.

1 oz. sloe gin
1 oz. gin
¾ oz. fresh lemon juice
2 teaspoons simple syrup
club soda, to top up
lemon slice, to garnish

Add all the ingredients, except the soda, to a shaker filled with ice. Shake sharply and strain into a highball glass filled with ice. Top with club soda, garnish with a lemon slice, and serve with two straws.

ginger champagne

The ginger combines conspiratorially with the champagne to create a cocktail that is delicate yet different enough to appease even the most sophisticated cocktail drinker.

2 thin fresh ginger slices
1 oz. vodka
champagne, to top up

Put the ginger in a shaker and press with a barspoon or muddler to release the flavor. Add ice and the vodka, shake, and strain into a champagne flute. Top with champagne and serve.

french 75

Named after the big artillery gun that terrorized the Germans during the First World War, rattling off rounds at a rate of 30 per minute. The popular variation on this drink was to mix cognac with the champagne, which would make sense since they were fighting in France!

¾ oz. gin
2 teaspoons fresh lemon juice
1 teaspoon simple syrup
champagne, to top up
lemon zest, to garnish

Shake the gin, lemon juice, and simple syrup with ice and strain into a champagne flute. Top with champagne and garnish with a long strip of lemon zest.

james bond

The James Bond is a variation on the Champagne Cocktail, using vodka instead of the more traditional brandy. The naming of this cocktail is a mystery to me since the eponymous spy liked his drinks shaken not stirred, as in this cocktail.

1 white sugar cube
2 dashes of Angostura bitters
1 oz. vodka
champagne, to top up

Place the sugar cube in a champagne flute and moisten with Angostura bitters. Add the vodka and top with champagne.

royal gin fizz

An offshoot of the original Gin Fizz, the Royal
Gin Fizz has become fashionable in its own right.
The substitution of soda with champagne helps
to make this cocktail special and lends it a little
extra fizz—surely no harm there!

1 egg white
2 oz. gin
1 oz. fresh lemon juice
1 teaspoon white sugar or ½ oz. simple syrup
champagne, to top up
lemon slice, to garnish

Put the egg white, gin, lemon juice, and sugar in a shaker
filled with ice, and shake vigorously. Strain into a highball
glass filled with ice. Top with champagne, and garnish
with a slice of lemon.

apricot royale

I would serve this one as shots to guests who I thought needed a bit of livening up! The fruity melody of flavors combines with the champagne to make this drink the perfect cure for the blues.

1 ¾ oz. apricot brandy
¾ oz. fresh lemon juice
¾ oz. simple syrup
a dash of peach bitters
a dash of orange bitters
champagne, to float
apricot slice, to garnish

Add all the ingredients, except the champagne, to a shaker filled with ice, shake sharply, and strain into a rocks glass filled with ice. Gently layer a float of champagne over the surface of the drink. Garnish with an apricot slice and serve.

metropolis

The Metropolis was a logical creation since the champagne and berry-flavored liqueur combination was such an obvious success in the Kir Royale. Adding vodka gave a kick to that same seductive mix of champagne and fruit flavors.

¾ oz. vodka
¾ oz. crème de framboise
champagne, to top up

Shake the vodka and the crème de framboise together with ice and strain into a martini glass. Top with champagne and serve.

mimosa

It is thought that Alfred Hitchcock invented this drink in an old San Francisco eatery called Jack's sometime in the 1940s, for a group of friends suffering from hangovers.

½ glass champagne
fresh orange juice, to top up

Pour the orange juice over half a flute-full of champagne and stir gently.

rossini

A great variation on the Bellini, the Rossini is spiced up with a little Chambord and a dash of orange bitters—two of a bartender's favorite cocktail ingredients.

½ oz. raspberry purée
1 teaspoon Chambord
2 dashes of orange bitters
champagne, to top up

Add the purée, Chambord, and bitters to a champagne flute and top gently with champagne. Stir gently and serve.

softies

iced tea

There is nothing more satisfying to make than a good Iced
Tea. I know, as I had a protracted debate about the best
way with a co-worker—it wasn't until he conceded that mine
was better than his that I really savored both the moment
and the drink!

4 tea bags
2 ½ quarts hot water
1 lemon, sliced
sugar, to taste

Add the tea bags to a pitcher of hot, but not boiling, water. Stir, take out
the tea bags, and let the tea cool and stand before adding fresh lemon
slices and chilling in the fridge. Once chilled, pour the tea into four highball
glasses filled with ice. Add sugar to taste, and serve with two straws.

virgin mojito

There's nothing in the manual that says cocktails with no alcohol in them should be low maintenance or one-dimensional. This one is a way of saying thank you to anyone who has taken on the noble role of designated driver for the night.

6 mint sprigs, plus 1 to garnish
1 teaspoon superfine sugar
2 lime wedges
club soda, to top up
a dash of simple syrup

Muddle the mint, sugar, and lime in a highball glass filled with ice. Fill with crushed ice, top with club soda and muddle gently. Add simple syrup to taste, garnish with a mint sprig, and serve with two straws.

cranberry
cooler

It's so simple, I defy anyone not to admit that this drink, when served ice cold and in the right proportions, is the only thing that almost beats a lemonade made just right!

soda water
cranberry juice
1 lime

Fill a tall highball glass with crushed ice. Pour in equal parts of soda water and then cranberry juice. Garnish with a squeeze of lime and serve with two straws.

st clement's

The name is taken from the English nursery rhyme "Oranges and Lemons said the bells of St. Clement's."

bitter lemon
fresh orange juice
lemon slice, to garnish

Build both ingredients (the bitter lemon first) in equal parts into a highball glass filled with ice. Stir gently, garnish with a lemon slice, and serve with two straws.

pussy foot

Try using freshly squeezed juice
for a slightly sweeter variation.

2 ½ oz. fresh orange juice
2 ½ oz. fresh grapefruit juice
2 ½ oz. pineapple juice
2 ½ oz. cranberry juice
a dash of grenadine
a dash of fresh lemon juice

Shake the ingredients well with ice and strain
into a highball glass filled with ice.

liver recovery

Between them, apples, strawberries, and bananas contain more nutrients and healing properties than I could fit on this page. What's even better, this drink tastes great!

2 green apples
6 fresh strawberries
1 banana

Peel, core, top and tail the assembled fruits, as necessary. Add the fruit to a blender filled with one scoop of crushed ice. Blend and pour into a small highball glass.

virgin mary

Since this variation of the Bloody Mary
is without vodka, I tend to go a bit
crazy on the spices to compensate!

10 oz. tomato juice
2 grinds of black pepper
2 dashes of Tabasco sauce
2 dashes of Worcestershire sauce
2 dashes of fresh lemon juice
1 barspoon horseradish sauce
celery stalk, to garnish

Shake all the ingredients over ice and strain
into a highball glass filled with ice. Garnish
with a celery stalk.

shirley temple

A thirst quencher for the very sweet-
toothed and, most appropriately,
named after the famous Hollywood
child actress.

¾ oz. grenadine
ginger ale or lemon soda, to top up
lemon slice, to garnish

Pour the grenadine into a highball glass filled
with ice and top with either ginger ale or
lemon soda. Garnish with a slice of lemon
and serve.

index

CONVERSION CHART

Measures have been rounded up or down slightly to make measuring easier. The key is to keep ingredients in ratio.

IMPERIAL	METRIC
½ oz.	10–12.5 ml
¾ oz.	15–20 ml
1 oz. (single)	25–30 ml
1½ oz.	35–40 ml
1¾ oz.	45–50 ml
2 oz. (double)	50–60 ml